YOUR KNOWLEDGE H,

Corporate Social Responsibility and its Impact on Consumer Buying Behaviour: A Case Study on H&M

Rositsa Ivanova

Bibliographic information published by the German National Library:

The German National Library lists this publication in the National Bibliography; detailed bibliographic data are available on the Internet at http://dnb.dnb.de.

ISBN: 9783346920485
This book is also available as an ebook.

© GRIN Publishing GmbH
Trappentreustraße 1
80339 München

Print and binding: Books on Demand GmbH, Norderstedt, Germany
Printed on acid-free paper from responsible sources.

The present work has been carefully prepared. Nevertheless, authors and publishers do not incur liability for the correctness of information, notes, links and advice as well as any printing errors.

GRIN web shop: https://www.grin.com/document/1380446

University of Economics - Varna

BACHELOR THESIS

TOPIC:

Corporate social responsibility and its impact on consumer
buying behaviour: A case study on H&M

Varna

2019

TABLE OF CONTENTS

LIST OF TABLES

LIST OF FIGURES

LIST OF ABBREVIATIONS

ANOVA   Analysis of Variance

CSR   Corporate Social Responsibility

EC   European Commission

EU   European Union

GHG   Greenhouse gas

H&M   Hennes & Mauritz

ISO   International Organisation for Standardization

UN   United Nations

I. INTRODUCTION

1.1 Background

The challenges of the XXI century affect every aspect of daily life and fashion industry is no exception. Being highly-intensive, clothing manufacturing becomes one of the first industries characterised as global with production and distribution lines spread out literally all over the world. While globalised activities are in general positively regarded, the down side of the clothing industry's internationality is that its production is being oriented to take place in countries with cheap workforce, varying government regulations, non-standardised employment and nature protection norms, causing thus a number of ethical issues. To balance out the controversy of the sector, clothing companies' management have been changing to embrace Corporate Social Responsibility (CSR) as a policy in attempt to find new solutions and respond to the rigorous demands from customers and stakeholders.

1.2 Tasks of the study and hypothesis

The current study's main objective is to identify a possible relationship between CSR and consumer behaviour and therefore, focuses on the conditions and situations where a company's CSR may lead to positive behavioural intentions among its customers. By doing so, of significance to the research is to perform the following tasks:

- To explore the evolution of CSR as a concept and how it is applied in the clothing industry, with particular focus on Carroll's pyramid of corporate social responsibility;
- To identify and analyse the motivators of implementing CSR in the clothing business and to outline the research methodology used to test the impact of CSR on consumer behaviour;

- To find out if by being socially responsible, a corporation in the retail sector influences consumer satisfaction and behaviour in terms of customers being willing to pay more for the brand's responsibility.
- To offer critical discussion of the CSR practices of one of the most-recognised multinational retail brands – Hennes & Mauritz (H&M) and to outline how social responsibilities have been regarded by the company.

CSR became a buzz word and gained prominence over the past decade, often used by companies to boost their image and to differentiate themselves and their goods to customers from competitors. Customer behaviour has also transformed due to increased level of income, overexposure to offerings and the rise of information technologies, clients becoming picky and critical and most importantly, demanding economic, legal, ethical and philanthropic responsibilities from corporations. Nevertheless, the study suggests that customers are selective when it comes to their demands and those shopping fast-fashion garments from brands such as H&M are unlikely to have CSR high on their agenda. This is due to the fact that this type of customers are in search of budgeted apparel and CSR is being associated by society with increasing the price of products and services. Therefore, the expectation is that the CSR policies led by the H&M Group would have low to medium uptake and the most popular ones would be sustainability programmes that generate direct value to customers, for example awards, discounts, or other types of incentives.

1.3 Subject, object and relevance of the research

The subject of the study is Corporate Social Responsibility applied to the clothing industry and the opportunities that the CSR concept creates for improvements, while the object is the world's second biggest clothing retailer – Hennes & Mauritz, known by the general public as H&M, infamous for its business strategy of fast fashion for which it is being severely criticised to have contributed to increased CO2 emissions, waste, and inequality with regard to labour rights and wages.

In order to narrow down the scope of the research and to avoid producing another paper that is too broad and does not clarify the challenges that fashion corporations face in building customer loyalty through social responsibility, the study focuses on the retail apparel industry only. This research aims to contribute to the existing literature that examines customer loyalty showcased in direct and indirect customer behaviour and analyses the relationship between CSR and the willingness to pay for CSR. The findings of the study would be beneficial for further exploration of marketing practices and techniques by giving insights into customers' decision-making process. Logically, appropriate policies, plans and business strategies could be tailored to attract new customers and to bring elicit positive responses from them. Ultimately, the results of the study could be used to justify change in the chosen firm's pricing or in similar companies that operate in the retail sector.

1.4 Methodology

The methods used to test the hypothesis and conduct the study were split into two stages, starting with an analysis of existing literature concerning the subject, focusing on academic resources that have become central when clarifying the notion of Corporate Social Responsibility, among which the works of Bowen, Carroll, Burke and Logsdon, Smith and lastly – the contribution on the matter of the European Commission. The definitions of these prominent for the subject of CSR researches were applied to discuss and assess how social responsibility is regarded by H&M and what kind of approaches it implements to offer solutions to the social and environmental problems it is facing. The second stage of the research is empirical – a survey, in order to test the positive behavioural intentions of consumers in response to the CSR campaigns of the selected enterprise. The two-stage methodology presents data from more than one point of view and thus, it aims to avoid certain limitations that are common for similar studies of the CSR practice, among which are biased perspective and ungrounded conclusions.

1.5 Structure of the research

The thesis consists of an introduction and three chapters, followed by a conclusion. The introduction demonstrates the key factors of researching Corporate Social Responsibility in the retail sector and provides the background to the subject along with a problem discussion and enlisting the tasks. Chapter One will present relevant theories from previous research, which main elements will be after that applied to the H&M Group's policies and programmes in attempt of the study to prepare a logical and justifiable presentation of the company's CSR. The last section of this chapter outlines the research methodology, design and approaches and discusses the reasons for their selection. The next chapter is a transitional one where CSR and retail are examined on the basis of the existing interdependences and the way social responsibilities define customer satisfaction, behaviour and willingness to pay. Chapter Three will provide the collected data, where presented theories will be evaluated towards the data and the hypothesis will be tested. Lastly, the paper enlists the research's findings and makes conclusions, following with the identified implications of the study and a proposal for future research.

II. CHAPTER ONE. THEORETICAL FOUNDATION AND EVOLUTION OF CORPORATE SOCIAL RESPONSIBILITY

2.1 Definition of Corporate Social Responsibility

The first definition of Corporate Social Responsibility appeared in 1953 and was presented by Howard Bowen, who is believed to be the founder of the doctrine of Corporate Social Responsibility.[1] Bowen defined the businesses' social responsibilities to be such as to fulfil the obligations, decisions and actions that had been marked as desirable by the society.[2] Approximately 30 years later, Archie Carroll's description of the notion became the first unified characterisation, stating that Corporate Social Responsibility encompasses multiple expectations of society – expectations of economic, legal, ethical and discretionary or philanthropic nature towards enterprises at a given point in time.[3] Carroll came up with the definition on the basis of other scholars' work and the reason his reading of the concept became more popular than other similar ones was that he had managed to provide a clearer and more concise conceptualisation that was vastly applicable under any context. Furthermore, he organised the main responsibilities a corporation has in a pyramid, in the base of which were positioned the economic responsibilities, followed by the legal responsibilities (the first two required by society), the ethical ones that were outside the law obligations and on the top sat the philanthropic responsibilities (the latter two desired by society, but not obligatory).

---

[1] Carroll, Archie B. A history of corporate social responsibility: concepts and practices. In A. M. Andrew Crane, D. Matten, J. Moon, and D. Siegel (Eds.), The Oxford handbook of corporate social responsibility. New York, Oxford University Press, 2008, p. 20.

[2] Bowen, Howard R. Social responsibilities of the businessman. University of Iowa Press, 1953, p. 6.

[3] Carroll, Archie B. A three-dimensional conceptual model of corporate performance. // Academy of management review, 1979, 4(4), p. 500.

In 1991, Donna Wood expanded Carroll's definition by adding three dimensions to explain better the essence of the concept:[4] 1) defined principles of CSR – legitimacy, public responsibility, and managerial discretion; 2) the process of CSR should include environmental assessment, management of stakeholders and problem-solving management; 3) the outcomes of CSR come in the form of social impact, programmes and/or policies.

The research of Lee Burke and Jeanne Logsdon in 1996 added a different aspect to the understanding of CSR as it focused on finding positive dependence between a firm's CSR and its financial performance.[5] This way the researchers evaluated the benefits through the finances prism of the implementation of CSR and highlighted the need of a strategic approach to achieve better business effectiveness. Throughout their study, Burke and Logsdon identified five strategic elements of CSR that they found essential: 1) centrality, in terms of compatibility of the chosen CSR with the corporation's mission, objectives and values; 2) specificity, understood as the ability to gain benefits for the company; 3) proactivity, which came down to the ability to foresee social trends and create policies around them; 4) voluntarism, in the form of discrete decision-making that is not provoked by requirements triggered by the outside environments; 5) visibility, that corresponds to the stakeholders' expectations.

As the corporate sector had been changing through the decades as well as the societal expectations, Corporate Social Responsibility was also modified to a certain extent to answer more closely to the needs of stakeholders and to the public interest in general. Therefore, Craig Smith tailored the definition of CSR to refer to the non-legal obligations of the company to all people that are somehow affected by its policies and practices. The ultimate goal of these

---

[4]Wood, Donna J. Corporate social performance revisited. // The Academy of Management Review, 1991, 16(4), p. 693.
[5]Burke, Lee, and Logsdon, Jeanne M. How corporate social responsibility pays off. // Long Range Planning, 1996, 29(4), pp. 495–502.

obligations is to minimise any harm on society and instead, enlarge the beneficial impact to involve a wider circle of audiences.[6] Realistically, for corporations to be able to achieve this level of CSR, they ought to include it as a priority in their corporate strategy and make it a long-term obligation to state their interdependence with the society's modern necessities.

Unlike in other places, in Europe the European Commission (EC) supports corporations with guiding policies and legislative definitions of CSR in order to unify the operative aspect of it and to enhance business activities with impact on society.[7] This leads to the provision of a definition of CSR that is developed on the basis of social and environmental integration of business operations and voluntary interaction with the respective stakeholders, which is presented in a brief and concise manner in the following phrase: "the responsibility of enterprises for their impacts on society." The Commission's conceptualisation is very close to Carroll's definition and also refers to the four types of firm's responsibilities – economic, legal, ethical and philanthropic, that has appeared in multiple literature sources since 1979.

[6]Smith, Craig. Changes in corporate practices in response to public interest advocacy and actions. In P. N. B. a. G. T. Gundlach (Ed.), Handbook of Marketing and Society. Thousand Oaks, 2001, p. 142.
[7]European Commission. Communication from the Commission to the European Parliament, the Council, the European Economic and Social Committee and the Committee of the Regions: A renewed EU strategy 2011-14 for Corporate Social Responsibility. Brussels, COM 2011, 681 final, p. 6. Retrieved from
https://www.employment.gov.sk/files/slovensky/ministerstvo/spolocenska-zodpovednost/new-communication-on-csr-2011-2014.pdf

1953: Bowen	• CSR: to fulfil the obligations, decisions and actions that have been marked as desirable by the society
1979: Carroll	• CSR: multiple expectations of society – of economic, legal, ethical and discretionary nature, towards enterprises at a given point in time • 1991 expanded by Wood: includes principles, definition of the process and outcomes
1996: Burke and Longsdon	• Finding positive dependence between a firm's CSR and its financial performance - 5 key strategic elements
2001: Smith	• CSR to answer to the needs of stakeholders and the general public

Figure 1. The process of defining Corporate Social Responsibility. Source: As per the researcher's collected data.

The definitions included in Figure 1. are only part of the many different ones published by CSR researchers, marketing specialists and business experts, and chosen to be presented due to being essential for understanding better the aspects of the current research.

2.2 Evolution of Corporate Social Responsibility from the Roman Empire to nowadays

Various are the corporate, political, social and public events that shaped the concept of Corporate Social Responsibility throughout its historical development and continue to change it, following the pace of modern corporate behaviour. Like other similar concepts, it is not possible to define the exact date when Corporate Social Responsibility appeared as an element of the business world, however, the majority of the analysts started mentioning it more actively in the 1930's and 40's,[8] which is a clear sign that some corporations began to act on their social responsibilities around that period. Other researchers, such as E. Chaffee, traced back the roots of social responsibility to the Roman Empire where it had appeared in the form of provision of asylums, homes, hospitals and orphanages.[9]That progressed to the Middle Ages in England and corporations continued to act as social enterprises later on in the XVI and XVII centuries to the extent that social responsibility was exported overseas to the newly formed United States of America. Christian religion had huge influence on the development of CSR, because it was pushing rich people to act on in order to reverse the moral decay of society mainly via philanthropy. The main social problems that were being resolved in Victorian times were around poverty, child and female labour,[10] which had led to the introduction of welfare programmes in Europe as well as in the USA.

In his work "A history of corporate social responsibility: concepts and practices", Archie B. Carroll described the evolution of welfare schemes in the last decades of the XVIII century and the beginning of the XIX century, that aimed at securing the employee's protection and for some companies, it went to the point of improving the quality of life of those workers.[11] What became a real issue in the dynamically urbanised world was the inability of farmers and small companies to keep up with the changing elements of modern economy, which led to the creation of labour unions and organisations that were focused on the promotion of values and the improvement of working conditions.[12] According to

---

[8]Agudelo, Mauricio Andrés Latapí, Jóhannsdóttir, Lára and Davídsdóttir, Brynhildur.A literature review of the history and evolution of corporate social responsibility. // International Journal of Corporate Social Responsibility,2019, 4:1, p. 1.
[9]Chaffee, Eric. The Origins of Corporate Social Responsibility. // University of Cincinnati Law Review, 2017, Vol. 85. Retrieved from SSRN: https://ssrn.com/abstract=2957820
[10]Harrison, Brian. Philanthropy and the Victorians. // Victorian Studies, 1966, 9(4), p. 353.
[11]Carroll, Archie B. Op. cit., 2008, p. 20.
[12]Agudelo, Mauricio Andrés Latapí, Jóhannsdóttir, Lára and Davídsdóttir, Brynhildur. Op. cit., p. 3.

Carroll's research,[13] business managers looked for ways to maintain the very much needed equilibrium between the expectations of clients and the realistic capacity of employees and that made them the so-called "middle-man" between both parties. By doing so, the corporations took on the responsibility to adapt a package of social and economic benefits that fitted well their individual profile, depending on the company's key objectives, industrial sector and target audiences.

The following decades marked by the First and the Second World Wars brought very little to the evolution of CSR and the corporations' actions were limited mainly down to philanthropy.[14] However, that gave time to society to adapt their vision on corporate behaviour and started seeing the large businesses as a concentration of great power with significant impact on people in the city. As a result, those corporations felt the necessity to respond to the public demand by adopting a set of principles that clearly show where they stand on the social responsibility path. The evolution stage in the 50's and 60's of the twentieth century was not so much about the development of the idea of social responsibility further, but more about finding a clear definition of the concept by the scholars that were researching it at the time. In general, the public awareness of the matter expanded and they became hugely concerned about the impact of the rapidly growing population, environmental pollution and depletion of the natural resources on Earth, as well as respecting to the human rights, civil and labour rights and environmental norms.[15]

The other aspect of the activity of the corporations that society sought responsibility from was in those cases when companies were somehow involved

---

[13]Carroll, Archie B. Op. cit., p. 2008, 23.
[14]Ibid.
[15]Du Pisani, Jacobus A. Sustainable development – historical roots of the concept. // Environmental Sciences, 2006, 3(2), p. 83.

in war or violated civil rights through their production.[16] That provoked people not only to oppose their production, but led to massive rallies. Slowly, CSR became a response to the main problems that society was experiencing at the time and therefore, corporations needed to take a stand in relation to ongoing social, economic and political debates. The more profitable the companies were, the higher the expectations of the society were.

Following on the CSR's development in the 1950's and 60's, Clarence Walton expanded the idea of the social positioning of businesses and suggested that they should reflect on politics, education, social welfare and even on the happiness of the employees.[17] Eventually, that would have the potential to contribute to the social improvement, limiting the extent of the pursuit of economic benefits only. Simultaneously, while some scholars were going deeper into the interdependence between economics and social responsibility of business, others like Milton Friedman were arguing that this approach was extremely unsuitable and social impact of enterprises should be limited to the pursuit of economic gains and going outside those endeavours would be unjustified.[18]

For the next decade, the public did not witness significant advance on CSR from corporations, except for more philanthropic activities, and that steered to building up on the distrust in them and more demonstrations.[19] Only in the last few years of the decade and the beginning of the next one, the contact between society and businesses deepened and businesses assumed broader responsibilities, following up the lead of the public and their needs rather than the other way round, that is, corporations to decide on the social policy they wanted

---

[16]Agudelo, Mauricio Andrés Latapí, Jóhannsdóttir, Lára and Davídsdóttir, Brynhildur. Op. cit., p. 4.
[17]Walton, Clarence. Corporate social responsibilities. United States of America, Wadsworth Publishing Company, 1967.
[18]Friedman, Milton. Capitalism and freedom. United States of America, University of Chicago Press, 1962.
[19]Agudelo, Mauricio Andrés Latapí, Jóhannsdóttir, Lára and Davídsdóttir, Brynhildur. Op. cit., p. 5.

to shine more light on. In this period some of the most renowned social oriented businesses were created and immediately attracted major attention from the public, such as the Body Shop in the UK (focused on products that have not been tested on animals, made by sustainable ingredients) and Ben & Jerry's in the USA (promoting their sustainably sourced products, mainly milk, the reduce of carbon emissions and children's protection)[20].These two examples demonstrated that companies were getting more and more involved into the required policies to manage corporate social responsibility and that was happening not because they were feeling pressure to do so, but due to their own individual approach on how they wanted to deliver their business. Slowly, other companies started to adopt the same attitude and sooner after that corporate social responsibility became the new trend,[21] without being clear which of the companies were doing it due to their managers' own perceptions, and which because the society expected them to do so.

The 1980's brought in new aspects of CSR in terms of a series of legislation changes in the UK and USA in order to reduce the pressure on companies that were experiencing the negatives of the world inflation.[22] Therefore, by aiming to maintain a free market, the State in many countries reduced the regulations applicable to private corporations, including tax and corporate behaviour expectations. Despite the fact that law was not as strict as before, different interest groups continued to look into corporate ethics and the business responsibility to stakeholders, employees and consumers. In 1980, Thomas Jones examined CSR as a decision making process, which presented its operational characteristics and thus, various CSR frameworks, models and methods followed.[23]They were in line

---

[20]Socially Responsible Causes Ben & Jerry's Has Advocated for. Ben & Jerry's Website, 2014. Retrieved fromhttps://www.benjerry.com/whats-new/2014/corporate-social-responsibility-history
[21]Carroll, Archie. B. Corporate social responsibility: The centerpiece of competing and complementary frameworks. // Organizational Dynamics, 2015, 44(2), p. 88.
[22]Agudelo, Mauricio Andrés Latapí, Jóhannsdóttir, Lára and Davídsdóttir, Brynhildur. Op. cit., p. 7.
[23]Jones, Thomas. Corporate social responsibility revisited, redefined. // California Management Review, 1980, 22(3), pp. 59–67.

with the growing concerns around environment conservation and protection, discrimination at the workplace, consumer rights, health and safety insurance provisions for employees and as a whole, the quality of work life, the challenges of living in the city and controversial practices adopted by internationally operating corporations.[24]

The events that were marked by the processes of globalisation of all aspects of life added an international perspective to the concept of CSR. The many new international bodies and the law documents they had produced set up higher standards with regard to corporate behaviour.[25] Due to the fact that very often corporations operated in several countries, they were facing very diverse working environments and that necessitated for them to strengthen their regulatory frameworks. The task was not that easy, because they existed with increasing international competition and certain expectations towards their reputation.

The first two decades of the XXI century are distinguishable by the remarkably quick expansion of CSR and the continuous academic research on its strategic approaches.[26]Also, to the development of CSR contributed the United Nations (UN) Global Compact attempting to fill in the gaps of governmental norms and regulations in the areas of human rights, social concerns and environmental challenges by creating an instrument that would be responsible to insert shared international values into the corporate markets. It is important to be clarified that United Nations Global Impact was never meant to be made functional for CSR only, but to create an integral corporate culture which long-term aims look at human rights, labour organisation and rights, preservation of environment and wildlife. The actions of the European Union (EU) came in slightly afterwards with the so-called Green Paper or "Promoting a European

---

[24]Carroll, Archie B. Op. cit., p. 2008, 36.
[25]Agudelo, Mauricio Andrés Latapí, Jóhannsdóttir, Lára and Davídsdóttir, Brynhildur. Op. cit., p. 7.
[26]Agudelo, Mauricio Andrés Latapí, Jóhannsdóttir, Lára and Davídsdóttir, Brynhildur. Op. cit., p. 9.

framework for Corporate Social Responsibility", which focused on promoting the environmental challenges that nations and their businesses were facing. The first step taken by the EU was done in 2001 and 10 years later, after a series of campaigns, the EU approach to CSR was to see it as a responsibility of corporations to control their impact on society.[27] In 2011, a renewed EU strategy for the period 2011-2014 was published to tackle the aspects of Corporate Social Responsibility and responsible business conduct with particular focus on working conditions, human rights, health, the environment, innovative practices, education and training.[28] One of the strategy's objectives was to demonstrate that the EU public authorities support and encourage businesses to conduct their production and operations in a responsible manner. Following up on its main strategy, the Commission issued an action plan for the period after 2014 on human rights and democracy and promoted further the United Nations global impact, 2030 agenda for sustainable development and the ISO 26000 guidance on social responsibility.

A European document with particular importance is the Enterprise 2020 Manifesto with the role to direct businesses towards adhering to Europe's sustainable economy and generating value in five main aspects:[29] 1) impact on society via business practices that are sustainable and responsible; 2) membership engagement and satisfaction in line with the work in Europe on CSR; 3) financial stability; 4) engaging employees on individual basis through investment in their professional and personal developments as well as on team basis, improving thus

[27] European Commission. Corporate social responsibility: a new definition, a new agenda for action.(MEMO/11/732, MEMO/11/734 and MEMO/11/735). European Commission Website, 2011. Retrieved from http://europa.eu/rapid/press-release_ MEMO-11-730_en.htm
[28] European Commission. Industry: Corporate Social Responsibility & Responsible Business Conduct. European Commission Website, 2011. Retrieved from https://ec.europa.eu/growth/industry/corporate-social-responsibility_en
[29] CSR Europe. CSR Europe - 20 years of business-policy interaction driving the CSR movement. CSR Europe Website, 2016. Retrieved from https://www.csreurope.org/history

the organisational capacity; 5) environmental impact that is well-documented and measured in order to determine the areas of improvement.

It was at this point of the CSR evolution that scholars became explicit in stating that social responsibility should be an integral part of the corporations' strategy and a long-term element of the relationship between business and society. According to Geoffrey Lantos, in 2000's CSR evolved in a way that it was understood to be crucial for the company's plans to generating profits, which meant that only those socially responsible activities that would bring financial benefits were to be taken under consideration, ignoring the holistic approach if not profitable.[30]Later on, many more analysts reviewed CSR through the lenses of strategic commitment of the company and it became part of the overall understanding of the concept. Strategic CSR relates to brand management and maintains legitimacy in the world of branding, that is no longer limited by national borders. Furthermore, strategic CSR is a way for a company to improve its competitiveness, to define its values and match them with its productivity and to the social context in which it operates. When the company manages to 'export' its internal values to the external world, that is, to customers and stakeholders, and eventually measures the impact by the company's strategic dimensions, it will have succeeded in gaining recognition and competitive advantage as compared to the other competing businesses in the sector. The added benefits of creating value for a corporation are the generation of new opportunities through the constant drive for improvement of strategic CSR and meeting the social demands, which automatically means acquiring better positions and recognition by the target audiences. By assessing the economic benefits of the corporation and those of the stakeholders, however, it raises the question who pays the price for the companies' holistic activities.

---

[30]Lantos, Geoffrey P. The boundaries of strategic corporate social responsibility. // Journal of Consumer Marketing, 2001, 18(7), pp. 595–632.

The creation of shared value was further explored by Michael Porter and Mark Kramer, who saw the business evolution to simultaneously improve the economic and social conditions of the communities in which a given corporation exists.[31] In other words, by aiming to economically progress, corporations also brought advantages to the society in the form of policies and operating practices. The view of Porter and Kramer on creating shared value could be seen as too idealistic, because of their suggestion that the purpose for a business to exist in the first place should be to create shared value. This is achievable by reconceiving the company's production, by redefining its meaning and positioning in the value chain, and by taking part in industry clusters. Even if corporations do not go that further ahead so they do not put CSR in the very centre of their existence and operational matters, assuming new responsibilities that are aimed at improving the social context is enough and an example of belonging to the third generation of CSR as per N. Leila Trapp's theory.[32]

2.3 Research methodology

One of the first models of Corporate Social Responsibility was presented by William Frederick in 1960 in attempt to balance out the increasing economic power of large scale corporations.[33] Frederick proposed corporations to adopt social responsibility policies based on five key elements: 1) to have a criteria for the value of economic production and distribution; 2) to incorporate the latest achievements in management and administration; 3) to take into consideration the historical and cultural distinctive characteristics with regard to the relevant

---

[31]Porter, Michael and Kramer, Mark. Creating shared value. // Harvard Business Review 2011, (January-February), p. 2.
[32]Trapp, N. Leila Corporation as climate ambassador: Transcending business sector boundaries in a Swedish CSR campaign. // Public Relations Review, 2012, 38(3), pp. 458–465.
[33]Frederick, William. The growing concern over business responsibility. // California Management Review, 1960, 2(4), pp. 54–61.

social context; 4) to recognise the importance each individual business and its leader has to perform a role within society; 5) to acknowledge that social behaviour is a result of deliberate actions and does not come automatically. In relation to Fredrick's first element, two decades later Tuzzolino and Armandi suggested a rationale for assessing the enterprise's socially responsible performance in the form of a five-point criteria – 1) profitability; 2) organisational safety; 3) affiliation and industry context; 4) market position and competitiveness; and 5) self-actualization.[34]

As much research is interested to investigate the cultural aspects that come into play in relation to CSR, the literature review that was conducted in preparation for the current research has shown that some of them tend to compare the customer reactions to the same enterprise in differing cultural and national contexts, while others compare the way it is CSR is perceived by people across various regions. For example, Isabelle Maignan studied responses of European consumers (French and German) compared to US consumers, and Sofie Mälstad and Carin Byström tested the responses of Spanish and Swedish consumers to the CSR strategies with focus on two major brands – Zara and H&M. Both researches were based on Carroll's pyramid and the four layers that construct it, having organised their hypotheses on the cultural foundations in the different countries. The empirical aspect of both studies laid on measuring surveys and a 7-point scale (from strongly disagree to strongly agree) developed by Isabelle Maignan and O.C. Ferrell in 2000.[35] Furthermore, according to Mohammed Y. A. Rawwas, culture should be viewed as the most important variable with influence on the consumer decision-making and ethics.[36]

---

[34]Tuzzolino, F., and Armandi, B. R. A need-hierarchy framework for assessing corporate socialresponsibility. The Academy of Management Review, 1981, 6(1), pp. 21–28.
[35]Maignan, Isabelle and Ferrell, O. C. Measuring Corporate Citizenship in Two Countries: The Case of the United States and France.// Journal of Business Ethics,2000, 23, pp. 283-297.
[36]Rawwas, Mohommed Y. A. Culture, personality and morality: A typology of international consumers' ethical beliefs. // International Marketing Review, , 2001, 18(2), p. 188.

Modern studies that examine different aspects of CSR tend to use complex methods that include interactions of variables, scenario-based manipulations and various scales to analyse data by averaging and forming indexes. The analysis of variance (also known as ANOVA) is one of the commonly used statistical methods and found suitable by the majority of researchers of CSR due to its associated estimation calculations utilised to outline differences among individual responses in a sample. The studies of Yelena Tsarenko and Dewi Tajib on "Consumers' forgiveness after brand transgression" and of Aristides I. Ferreira and Inês Ribeiro "Are you willing to pay the price?" are examples where the testing method has been applied. Furthermore, inferential statistics and T-tests (to assess the sample standard deviation) are often used to test the impact of demographics on certain factors as well as the reliability of the questions (usually by the Cronbach's alpha).[37]

The current study has chosen to develop its methodology in two stages: 1) critical analysis of a case study tested against the individual elements of the conceptualisations included in the first part of this chapter where the elements of CSR have been defined; 2) empirical study to test the positive behavioural intentions of consumers in response to the CSR campaigns of the selected enterprise. Therefore, the purpose of the study is combined – explanatory – in attempt to identify plausible casual networks shaping CSR in the enterprise, and exploratory – aimed at discovering important variables and generating hypotheses for further research. Typical for explanatory and exploratory research is data collection through a case study, document analysis and survey questionnaire, which is applicable for this research as well.

With respect to the combined purpose of the paper, the research approach is also a mixture of qualitative and quantitative methods. Although the

---

[37]Levine, David M., Berenson, Mark L. and Stephan, David. Statistics for managers using Microsoft Excel (Vol. 660). Upper Saddle River, New Jersey, Prentice Hall, 2008.

complexity of the research becomes greater when both approaches are applied, the unstructured, but elaborative techniques of the qualitative measurement allow to develop stable interpretations, proved by numeric indicators and thorough empirical assessments. The quantitative measurements are completed after collecting the necessary information through questioning of a number of respondents.[38] The number was not set, however, the highest possible number of surveyed participants was aimed that could have been achieved within the limitations of the research. The respondents were asked questions about their behaviour, attitudes, personal knowledge, awareness and motivations. In general, questionnaires are preferred because of their simplicity to carry out online and administer, data is reliable, easily checkable and analysed. The particular questionnaire does not have open questions, which limits respondents with the type of information they might want to share on the subject. Although some analysts see the questionnaire type of research method to be far too structured due to the fixed response questions, for the needs of the research this is the most suitable approach and the limitations will be taken into consideration and commented on at the end of the paper where suggestions for further research on the topic will be made. The set of questions is short and all questions are formulated in a clear, concise manner, replicating similar questionnaires that have been applied for other enterprises to test customer views on their CSR.

The questionnaire survey was conducted by mail and electronic interviews. A small part of the correspondents were emailed the questions – those were the people who did not feel comfortable to fill in the survey online and in English. The rest of the people were invited to participate via the researcher's social media channels (a link to the survey was shared) and transferred to Google Forms, where the questionnaire had been created in electronic version and made available to fill

---

[38]Mälstad, Sofie and Byström, Carin. Consumers' Perception of CSR within the Fashion Industry. Luleå University of Technology, 2013, p. 24.

in. Common advantages and disadvantages of the selected research approach are presented in Table 1. below.

Factor	Mail survey	Internet/Social media survey
Speed of data collection	Available by email once sent, but the researcher has limited control and needs to enter the responses manually into the statistics file; not too intrusive	Available at all times; statistics are updated immediately; not too intrusive
Geographic flexibility	Worldwide access	Worldwide access
Respondent cooperation	Variable as it depends how often the respondent checks their mail inbox and of the quality of the questionnaire's design	Social media channels promote participation and the more people take the questionnaire, the more popular it becomes
Versatility of questioning	Not versatile and the format is limited to several options	Not hugely versatile and the format is limited to several options supported by the survey portal
Questionnaire length	Same length for both versions and depending on the actual questions	Same length for both versions and depending on the actual questions
Item non-response rate	Low to medium	Medium to High
Possibility for respondent misunderstanding	Relatively high as the researcher is not present and relies on the questions being clear enough with no necessity for further elaboration	Relatively high as the researcher is not present and relies on the questions being clear enough with no necessity for further elaboration
Degree of researcher	No influence as the researcher is not present; partiality is reduced	No influence as the researcher is not present; partiality is reduced

influence on answers		
Anonymity of respondent	Not applicable because the researcher will be able to see the details of the respondent from the incoming email unless they are being supported by a third person	It depends on the respondent if they would prefer to remain anonymous or to reveal their identity to the researcher
Ease of call-back or follow-up	Easy, but time-consuming	Impossible, unless the respondent has revealed their identity and shared contact details at the end of the survey
Cost	No costs involved	No costs involved
Disadvantages	Problems with email addresses; limited ability for the researcher to gain insight into the responses	Failure due to technical problems; limited ability for the researcher to gain insight into the responses
Special features	Respondents can fill in the questionnaire at the most convenient time for them, therefore, give high-quality answers	Internet based sites for surveys provide extra features such as statistically derived graphics in real time

Table 1. Strengths and weaknesses of email and Internet based questionnaires. Source: Adapted from Sofie Mälstad and Carin Byström, Consumers' Perception of CSR within the Fashion Industry.

The questions that were included in the questionnaire had been selected as a result of extensive literature review of other similar studies. The leading factors that shaped the questions and defined their essence were the intention to attract as many respondents as possible and to have a validated and reliable study with questions that had already been tested. The survey was prepared in two language versions – in English and in Bulgarian, in order to reach diverse respondents and due to the fact that the research is located in Bulgaria, while the paper is being written in English. The questionnaire contained eight questions, two regarding respondents' demographics (age and gender), four relating to the respondents' knowledge, personal support and evaluation of corporate social responsibility and two questions to measure consumers' knowledge and responsiveness to H&M's CSR. The survey is illustrated in full in English in Appendix I. All questions were closed ones, but some of them were multiple choice and others – check boxes, which allowed correspondents to mark as many of the listed answers as applicable to them.

In this study the respondents that were studied are of different nationality, gender and relatively various backgrounds, however, the majority of people are middle class, working people. It can be argued that the study represents a random selection of respondents. With respect to time constraints, the survey was sent out and the collection of responses closed after two weeks to allow the preparation of the paper in a timely manner. The collected answers are not too many, which could be treated as the survey not being precise enough, but the smaller proportion of answers still gives reliable measures, mainly due to the construction of the questions and its close-end answers.

The way the collected data will be presented is using the descriptive statistics, that is, describing, displaying and organising the collected data through using graphs, tables and summary measurements.

III. CHAPTER TWO. CORPORATE SOCIAL RESPONSIBILITY IN THE RETAIL INDUSTRY

3.1 CSR in Retail

To understand the current situation of Corporate Social Responsibility in the retail industry as per 2019, it is necessary to refer to previously conducted studies and analyses, especially those that have somehow contributed with insights on the environment which H&M operates in. The CSR literature is not uniform regarding how CSR affects the retail industry across different brands and countries and its influence on the consumers' willingness to pay, regardless of the vastness of studies that look at consumers' responses to branding and attempts to provide understanding about the factors that affect consumer behaviour.[39]

Increasing number of corporations in retail engage with CSR initiatives with intention to gain advantage over their direct competitors by relating to consumers on emotional and social level. Other popular reasons for a firm to embed CSR in its operations are corporate reputation and contributing to the image of good corporate citizenship.[40] Usually, the policies that are aimed at popularising the firm's CSR are shaped in a way to build brand equity and strengthen the relationship and loyalty between consumers and the brand.[41] It is important to emphasise that more often than not the consumer relates to the brand and not to the company, feeling loyal to the idea that shapes up the brand and at the same time knows very little about the company's CSR strategy. Furthermore, whenever consumers are aware of a company's or brand's CSR initiatives, the

---

[39]Ferreira, Aristides I. and Ribeiro, Inês. Are you willing to pay the price? The impact of corporate social (ir)responsibility on consumer behaviour towards national and foreign brands. //Journal of Consumer Behaviour, 2017, 16, p. 63.
[40]Tsarenko, Yelena and Tojib, Dewi. Consumers' forgiveness after brand transgression: the effect of the firm's corporate social responsibility and response. // Journal of Marketing Management, 2015, Vol. 31, Nos. 17-18, pp. 1855.
[41]Bhattacharya, C. B., and Sen, Sankar. Consumer-company identification: A framework for understanding consumers' relationships with companies. // Journal of Marketing, 2003, 67(2), pp. 76–88.

intention to repurchase proportionally increases.[42] Based on those studies, one can conclude that the CSR activities and information campaigns positively impact the sales of products and services.

The abovementioned observations, however, do not mean that consumers are actually aware of the corporations' CSR strategies. The study of Alan Pomering and Sara Dolnicar from 2009 showed that no more than 20% of consumers care to receive regular information of CSR marketplace information.[43] Even those who are interested in the issue, shared that they have some doubts on the legitimacy of the ongoing CSR initiatives and expressed scepticism with regard to the firm's motives. Often consumers who demonstrate willingness to support socially responsible enterprises feel unsure about their knowledge on the matter and on the characteristics they ought to be aware of. Consumers in Western society get regularly exposed to terms such as fair trade, responsible consumerism, recycling and reusing, sustainability in relation to purchasing decisions.[44] Responsibility to all those terms, trends and policies do not get identical response and consumers needs vary from region to region and country to country even within the European Union.

By referring to the academic inquiries of Tom Brown and Peter Dacin (conducted in 1997) and of Sankar Sen and C. B. Bhattacharya (conducted in 2001), it has been found that negative perception on a business due to weak or misleading CSR is far more influential and long-lasting than creating and maintaining positive perception among consumers. CSR policies have the potential to influence purchase intentions directly and indirectly, regardless if it is bad reputation or a successfully led CSR strategy.[45] CSR with direct effect takes

---

[42]Lindgreen, A., Xu, Y., Maon, F., and Wilcock, J. Corporate social responsibility brand leadership: A multiple case study. // European Journal of Marketing, 2012, 46(7/8), pp. 965–993.
[43]Pomering, Alan and Dolnicar, Sara. Assessing the prerequisite of successful csr implementation: Are consumers aware of CSR initiatives? // Journal of Business Ethics, 2009, 85 (Suppl. 2), pp. 285–301.
[44]Mälstad, Sofie and Byström, Carin. Op. cit., p. 4.
[45]Ibid.

place when the corporate context is shaped in a way to create purchasing intentions, while the indirect influence comes when the consumer is aware of the enterprise's CSR work but nothing in the advertising and marketing stimulates him to buy more only because the product or the service is socially responsible. Ultimately, a clever CSR campaign is the one that encourages consumers to demonstrate responsiveness to enterprises' efforts to be socially responsive and make informed purchasing decisions.

3.2 Willingness to pay for CSR

As generalised by Geoffery Sprinkle and Laureen Maines, the implementation and maintenance of Corporate Social Responsibility strategy and its activities always entails additional costs for the firm's production.[46] In the competitive and globalised world it is very unlikely that a firm's CSR alone will create a strong stimulus to buy. The willingness to buy is determined by a combination of factors and they can only increase the consideration for buying, without guaranteeing the actual purchase. The consumer specific factors that navigate the customer's purchase are divided into three groups:[47]

- Core factors: information and personal concern, which leads to the possibility of CSR to be taken into consideration, but only if the consumer is aware of the firm's work with CSR;
- Central factors: assessment of the financial situation from the buyer's perspective (sufficiency of funds), level of information

---

[46]Sprinkle, Geoffrey B., and Maines, Laureen A. The benefits and costs of corporate social responsibility. // Business Horizons, 2010, 53(5), p. 445.
[47] Öberseder, Magdalena, Schlegelmilch, Bobo B. and Gruber, Verena. "Why Don't Consumers Care About CSR?": A Qualitative Study Exploring the Role of CSR in Consumption Decisions. // Journal of Business Ethics, 2011, 104, pp. 449-460.

(extent of knowledge about an enterprise's work) and the type of information (positive / negative impact on the consumer);

- Peripheral factors: credibility of the enterprise's CSR, including the company's image and influence of friends and family.

The involvement of corporations that belong to the retail industry in business practices defined by the principles of Corporate Social Responsibility supposedly demonstrates intentions towards increased customer loyalty and confidence in customers' willingness to pay higher prices.[48] It is equivocal though if customers in fact react in the way businesses expect or are led by other principles and ideas that motivate their everyday choices. The survey of Forbes from 2011 for example showed that customers are not willing to pay more for services and products and instead expect sustainability to be the baseline for all sorts of businesses.[49] Forbes found that the down side of creating green solutions is not only the refuse of customers to pay more for it as in comparison with the "non-green" solutions, but it provokes them to ask the question how the other products of the company, that are not marked as sustainable, have been produced. The presence of CSR policy never guarantees the purchase itself. However, if sustainability lacks from the portfolio of the company, then the customer would rather go for a competitor that clearly is taking social responsibility as a must in their activities. The balance of information available to the general public on a company's CSR is also important when a customer is deciding whether to buy or not – too much information and advertising on the matter can have the opposite effect and be perceived as aggressive.

---

[48]Yuen, Kum Fai, Thai, Vinh V. and Wong, Yiik Diew.Are customers willing to pay for corporate social responsibility? A study of individual-specific mediators. // Total Quality Management, 2016, Vol. 27, No. 8, p. 912.
[49]Unruh, Gregory. No, Consumers Will Not Pay More for Green. The CSR Blog Contributor Group, Forbes Website, 2011. Retrieved fromhttps://www.forbes.com/sites/csr/2011/07/28/no-consumers-will-not-pay-more-for-green/#6c71a1703b28

Another aspect of the willingness and respectively the lack of willingness to pay is the observed by scientists assumptions that socially responsible products and services tend to cost more than standard products and services that are not marketed as responsible. This could be true if the company includes the CSR work into the price, for example all products marked as fair trade, but this practice is not applied exclusively to all the production coming from sustainable producers. Although limited, studies in this respect show that if the price difference is relatively small, the customer will still buy the product on the grounds that it has been responsibly derived.[50]

3.3 Interdependence between CSR and customer satisfaction

A number of studies (for example the one of Eugene Anderson and Vikas Mittal from 2000)[51] suggest that customers are not always concerned with the corporation's overall strategy and all of its specifics, however, satisfaction should be achieved when the company is serving these customers. Only after that the firm can seek a suitable opportunity to introduce its CSR programme, hoping to maintain the positive behavioural attitude of the clients and extend it to CSR with premium added value that would stimulate the customers to be willing to pay more. Achieving a high level of customer satisfaction is an ultimate goal of each retailer and that is seen as an overall evaluation of a service or a product as well as the customer's experience with the company.[52] There are a number of ways customer satisfaction can be improved, mainly through the management of company's services, but in recent years of particular importance is the so-called

---

[50] Öberseder, Magdalena, Schlegelmilch, Bobo B. and Gruber, Verena. Op. cit., p.457.
[51] Anderson, Eugene W. and Mittal, Vikas. Strengthening the satisfaction-profit chain. // Journal of Service Research, 2000, 3(2), pp. 107–120.
[52] Yuen, Kum Fai, Thai, Vinh V. and Wong, Yiik Diew. Are customers willing to pay for corporate social responsibility? A study of individual-specific mediators. // Total Quality Management, 2016, Vol. 27, No. 8, p. 913.

holistic management, where psychological perception becomes central. The psychological approach in buyer behaviour analysis has cognitive, emotional, behavioural and relational aspects and usually those are stimulated through marketing techniques, advertising being the most popular one.[53] Seeing an advertisement is the strongest stimulus for the customer to start thinking about the product because visuals are immediately registered by the brain, they bring loads of information and looking is a human activity performed with relatively no efforts and minimum energy. It takes only one visual from the entire advertisement to affect the viewer subconsciously, that is why advertising is always associated with brightness, colours, dynamics and illustrative images. The cognition kicks in when that single visual has been registered and perceived by the customer to eventually arouse the motivation to purchase the advertised item.

When it comes to including CSR into advertising, such as the firm's sustainable and memorable values, it is believed that contribution to the environment and discussing societal issues are the most powerful to influence the consumption decision. Partially, the reason for that is the fact that those topics have been widely discussed and the general public easily relates to them, understands the context and can associate themselves with the tackled problem by the corporation. The more complex the firm's CSR is, the less supporters will abide to it simply because not that many people will recognise the issue as their own. As a consequence, when the corporation's practices of CSR are recognised and appraised, customer satisfaction will increase. This interdependence was identified and theorised with four different theories – value theory, equity theory, institutional theory, and corporate identity theory, all presented in the study of

[53]Jakštienė, Sandra, Susnienė. Daliaand Narbutas, Valdas. The Psychological Impact of Advertising on the Consumer Behaviour. // Communications of the IBIMA, 2008,No. 3, pp. 50-55. Retrieved fromhttps://ibimapublishing.com/articles/CIBIMA/2008/521523/521523.pdf

Kum Fai Yuen, Vinh V. Thai and Yiik Diew Wong (see Table 2.) to prove that CSR has a positive direct impact on customer satisfaction.

Theory	Customer satisfaction	CSR relation
Perceived value theory	Derived from a product or a service's attributes	An attribute to the product/service that creates functional, emotional and social connection with the customer; this way values created as a result of the firm's CSR augment the customer evaluation of the corporation and other of its products/services.
Equity theory	Derived from the principle of fair treatment of individuals	CSR activities can enhance customer satisfaction, especially those focused on fair treatment of employees and consequently, fair treatment of customers.
Institutional theory	Derived from the perception that customers are members of a society and as such, they are affected by a firm's operations that have direct impact on them and on the environment they exist in.	Contribution to the environment and the society combined with the consumption experience is expected to meet the customers' expectations and result in greater customer satisfaction.
Corporate identity theory	Derived from creating positive branding of the firm	Creation of a brand that is widely associated with the company's CSR and customers can identify themselves with.

Table 2. Customer satisfaction theories linked with the concept of CSR. Source: Adapted from Kum Fai Yuen, Vinh V. Thai and Yiik Diew Wong, A study of individual-specific mediators.

It is a mistake to navigate customer satisfaction in isolation from customer loyalty, and the aforementioned theories in Table 2. clearly show this. Long-lasting customer satisfaction is almost always achieved through building deep commitment in the customer with a product or a service, causing repetitive behaviour of buying the same brand and product again in the future.[54] However, the company is expected to continuously provide the high level of service and maintain customer satisfaction on every occasion creating behavioural and attitudinal types of experiences. The goal of the corporation is to achieve true loyalty that can be irrational at times and reduces the price sensitivity, allowing for a wider range of price and customer experience tolerance. That is a very sensible equilibrium though and cannot be maintained for long periods of time – it lasts until the pricing gets underestimated and the positive features of the CSR overestimated.

---

[54]Oliver, Richard L. Satisfaction: A behavioral perspective on the consumer (2nd Ed.). New York, M.E. Sharpe, 2010, p. 434.

IV. CHAPTER THREE. THE CASE STUDY OF CSR IN H&M

There is no doubt that the globalised world has changed consumers' behaviour, their preferences, needs and reactions to events, blending in national culture differences and providing unstoppable stream of information available to people. In this context, businesses that operate in multinational environment are expected to maintain policies and programmes in line with international standards, but also to respond to all national specifics and uniform them in their everyday activities. Integrating CSR into a retail enterprise that is located in more than one country could be an extremely challenging task with crucial influence on the company's outlook and its perception by clients.

For the past decade, the retail sector has undertaken spectacular steps towards improving their social responsibility, but it is still subject to severe critics for abusing a number of environmental regulations, human rights and animal welfare and continues to be highly controversial. The brand of H&M is one of the global retailers that receives significant press attention and has been criticised for their CSR work. Despite the widespread information in the press of H&M's failure to meet consumers expectations on sustainability and social responsibility, it is unclear what the real consequences on the enterprise's 'wellbeing' are and how deeply that affected the achievement of their financial KPIs. It becomes even more challenging to find out what the cross-culture perceptions are, regardless if the scope is on the EU where supposedly the cultural differences are less distant or on a selection of countries in different continents.

History and background of H&M

H&M is one of the most popular and recognised fashion brands worldwide as per 2019 and this attracts the researcher's interest in assessing its CSR – the efforts that the company makes to improve its CSR behaviour and its consumers' perceptions on that. H&M dates back to 1947 when the first clothing store called 'Hennes' was opened by Erling Persson in Sweden to sell women's apparel.[55]It took several years until the company expanded outside of Sweden to Norway, followed by change of the name to Hennes & Mauritz that brought in men's and children's clothing to the company's portfolio. In 1974 H&M was listed on the Stockholm Stock Exchange which came to show that it was expanding and was considered one of the successful enterprises in Sweden at the time. The following decades were marked by quick expansion of the company to other European counties (UK, Germany, the Netherlands, Benelux, Austria, Scandinavia and France). Only in 2000 H&M extended their presence outside Europe, appearing in the US, but the decade was more about striking collaborations with some of the biggest designers in fashion than anything else. In the second half of the first decade of the 21st century, H&M began to operate online through the company's website - hm.com, that again was initially available only in Europe and later on the online service was provided in the rest of the company's markets.

To understand better the scope of H&M's activities, it is important to highlight that H&M is no longer a single firm, but a corporation with several brands, apart from H&M, such as COS, FaBric Scandinavien AB – Cheap Monday, Monki, Weekday, H&M Home, &Other Stories, Arket and AFound as well as a foundation that functions as a non-profit global organisation. In 2010, H&M presented for the first time their H&M Conscious Collection that is developed around the use of sustainable materials (organic cotton, recycled polyester). Next step in the sustainable behaviour of the corporation was the development of an incentive programme for its employees in the shape of investment shares (H&M Incentive Program – HIP). In 2013, H&M became the first fashion company that was collecting old textiles with the purpose to re-use

---

[55]H&M. Our History: The H&M group – the first 70 years. H&M Website, 2017, p. 104. Retrieved from https://about.hm.com/content/dam/hmgroup/groupsite/documents/en/Digital%20Annual%20Report/2017/Annua l%20Report%202017%20Our%20history.pdf

and recycle them – an initiative available in stores worldwide. In the following year, H&M launched their first denim apparel made of recycled fibres.In 2017 the corporation set ambitious sustainability goals that became indicative for the fashion sector – to use only recycled and sustainably derived materials by 2030, and to operate their value chain in a climate-positive manner no later than 2040.

4.1 Implementation and evolution of CSR practices in H&M

To examine the way CSR has been implemented in the practices of H&M, the study's starting point is to cross-reference it with the essential elements that comprise Corporate Social Responsibility as per the definitions outlined in Chapter One. The study seeks to conduct a critical analysis on the implementation and evaluation of the CSR in H&M by clarifying how the retail firm fulfils the obligations of economic, legal, ethical and discretionary nature marked as required and desirable by society.

Principles of CSR in H&M

The H&M's principles of the Corporate Social Responsibility strategy are scientific-based and centred around three main points:[56]

- Leading the change – promotion of innovation, transparency and sustainable actions as per the global indexes;
- Circular & renewable – applied to the product lines, materials and climate impact of the value chain;

---

[56]H&M Group. Sustainability Report 2017, 2017, p. 11. Retrieved from
https://about.hm.com/content/dam/hmgroup/groupsite/documents/masterlanguage/CSR/reports/2017%20Sustain
ability%20report/HM_group_SustainabilityReport_2017_FullReport.pdf

- Fair & equal – in relation to jobs and employees, achieving diversity and inclusiveness.

According to Interbrand, a brand building analyst company and known for preparing the most renowned global brand ranking every year, H&M scores under number 30 in the Best Global Brands 2018 Rankings.[57] The ranking includes only the brand of H&M, the leading retail clothing brand of H&M Group and categorises it as "one of the world's leading fashion companies". The data published by Interbrand, nevertheless, indicates that for the period from 2017 to 2018 H&M suffered decrease of profits by 18% and finished last year being estimated to cost 17 billion US dollars. The income figures come to reveal the *major economic responsibilities* that H&M Group has due to its impressive scale and global scope – as per 2018 the corporation has 4 968 stores in 71 independent markets and maintains e-commerce available in 47 independent markets. The number of employees contracted by H&M Group is more than 177 000, but this number goes much higher when the hundreds of thousands of people who work in any of the 2 383 supplier factories around the world are taken into consideration.[58]. Maintaining economic and financial sustainability clearly becomes the foundation of the enterprise and required by the society in order to be able to conform to the legal, ethical and philanthropic expectations as well.

The way sustainability is integrated into the analysed company and its performance is by measuring each central function and the individual brands included in the corporation on a set of sustainability Key Performance Indicators in combination with sales figures and customer satisfaction. H&M Group has developed an additional method to cross-reference and interlink the company's

---

[57]Interbrand. Best Global Brands 2018 Ranking: H&M, 2019. Retrieved from https://www.interbrand.com/best-brands/best-global-brands/2018/ranking/hm/
[58] H&M Group. Sustainability Report 2018, 2018, p. 10. Retrieved fromhttps://about.hm.com/content/dam/hmgroup/groupsite/documents/masterlanguage/CSR/reports/2018_Susta inability_report/HM_Group_SustainabilityReport_2018_%20FullReport.pdf

goals, standards and vision with the sustainability activities within the Change-making Programme, to ensure that sustainability would not be siloed and somehow get disconnected from the rest of its business priorities and ongoing activities.

Although Archie Carroll differentiated *legal* and ethical responsibilities, in the modern business world these often overlap and the differentiation between *complying with laws and regulations* and *performing in an ethical manner* responsibilities relating to human rights is difficult to make. It is almost impossible huge corporations such as H&M to not comply with legislation, regardless if it is domestic, regional or international. The pressures on global brands are huge and they are being scrutinised on a daily basis, which pushes them further to apply additional standards in order to demonstrate the level of their commitment to operate in a fair and equal manner. Competition is another factor to consider, therefore providing access to a fair compensation programme, maintaining a workplace that is safe and healthy as well as an environment free from discrimination and respect for each employee is an absolute must.

Several of H&M Group recent changes were created in order for the enterprise to be able to offer fair jobs for all in the entirety of the value chain of all the brands of the company, and due to legal changes in the UK that require employers with more than 250 employees on the territory of the UK to report details on their gender pay gap. The reported data in 2017 showed that the pay gap for the H&M's employees in the UK is only 3.94%, which is twice less than the average for retailers.

While the fairness in the UK and the rest of the EU is not so much of an issue, despite the existing discrepancies in certain areas, the situation in the production market countries is very different from that. The level of implementation of legislation with regard to civil and labour rights in many of the countries in Asia and South America is poor and that is caused by the simple fact that fairness at the workplace is not available to all. It is an ethical question for every company with similar characteristics to those of H&M to decide how they would like to approach this very serious problem and what realistically can be achieved that is within the businesses' reach and capabilities. Monitoring of the working conditions in supply chain factories is the first step forward for the fashion industry to tackle the problem with the lack of fairness at the workplace. This put the foundations for achieving improvement of health and safety policies and their actual applicability, regular employment and payment as per the national legislation. One of the most important objectives of these monitoring measures were to prevent child labour and other human rights violations, for example forced labour and any forms of human trafficking, that in many of the cases affect women the most.

Another critical element of the CSR work of the H&M Group has been to support a fair living wage. H&M Group does not perform the improvement of industrial relations on its own, but collaborates with other key players such as trade unions, influential businesses within the fashion industry, factory owners and governments as the challenge is too big even for a large scale corporation such as H&M. The most challenging aspects of this endeavour are related to the necessity that the amounts of the fair living wage need to be revised regularly, ideally on an annual basis, to negotiating fair wage with factory owners who produce garments of more than one brand in their factory, and to the inability of H&M Group to influence the actual wage of every single employee in the factories where apparel is being produced, despite the purchasing practices and the final price tag of every produced piece of clothing. Furthermore, the negotiations with factory owners and local governments are often prolonged and may not necessarily engage in the type of dialogue the H&M Group would like to have with them and on top of that, national specifics and individualities complicate the matter and require individual solutions that rarely can be replicated in full elsewhere.

The approach of H&M to the *ethical responsibilities* is linked with their work with the so-called changemakers or in other words – the people who are in the position to support the transformation of fashion into an ethical and sustainable industry. The directions of the corporation's sustainability strategy work by setting up goals, roadmaps, standards and policies, methods and by following up those through the collaboration with four main groups of changemakers: stakeholders & experts (to address specific challenges and included in the development of realistic long-term action plans), business partners (when raising up environmental and social standards applicable for the entire fashion industry), colleagues (inviting employees to contribute and using their individual talents and skills) and customers (inspiring them to make sustainable choices).[59]

Moreover, accelerating the changes to achieve full circularity in terms of greater recycling levels, sustainably and responsibly sourced materials, innovative design and longer lifespan of products that conforms to the societal expectations for ethical production is another type of ethical responsibilities that build on the legal responsibilities of the enterprise. Part of those objectives are dependent on the innovative and effective implementation of new technologies into the production cycle of H&M. This itself is a considerable challenge even for a profitable company as H&M because it requires financial investments in countries where economic challenges and realities are slightly different from those in advanced and developed Europe and North America.

The *philanthropic responsibilities* of H&M can be justified with the existence of H&M Foundation that operates as a non-profit global foundation

---

[59]H&M Group. Op. cit., 2017, p. 12-13.

with private funding provided by the company's owner and his family as well as by the founders of the enterprises that take part of the corporation and the main owners of the H&M group.[60] The foundation's mission is in line with the society's shared values and expectations that companies with the size of H&M group ought to act as good corporate citizens driving long-lasting and positive systematic changes of the living conditions and operations through investment in people, communities and innovative concepts.

The charitable dimension of H&M's sustainability work include several approaches, one of them being H&M CO:LAB. This is a think-tank within the company investing in companies that have the potential to add value to the business. In other words, H&M invests financial and technical resources into independent companies that can support them in developing the necessary technologies and solutions. Although the activity itself qualifies as philanthropic, it is questionable if that is really the case, since clearly it is sought to get added value to H&M's business. Pure philanthropic actions in the corporate sector is a very subjective matter and examples of such activities are often argued to be tied-up with business interests.

Another variation of the traditional philanthropy is taking action on behalf of customers and providing incentives that not only contribute to the CSR portfolio of H&M, but also create positive behaviour among customers and reward them for their sustainable actions. Among these are:[61] H&M - collection of unwanted garments and textiles regardless of their brand and condition with the purpose to be recycled, re-worn or reused and in return customers are rewarded with a voucher applicable to their next purchase at H&M; &Other Stories – same programme as in H&M in combination with collection of beauty products containers to be recycled for which customers get 10% off of their next

---

[60]H&M Group. Op. cit., 2017, p. 4.
[61]H&M Group. Op. cit., 2017, p. 27.

in-store purchase; Cheap Monday and Monki – collection of unwanted textiles to be reused or recycled and in turn customers receive a voucher for 10% off for the next time they make a purchase. These initiatives added up to a considerable increase of the total share of recycled or other sustainably sourced materials by the H&M Group – in 2013 that was 11%, increasing to 20% in 2015 and reaching 35% in 2017.

The pyramid shaped Figure 2. summarises all of the above described responsibilities and demonstrates visually the logic of Carroll's theory of CSR, applied to the case of H&M. Economic responsibilities lay the foundation for all the other layers and unless these requirements have been fully satisfied, the rest cannot be achieved. Although it is a pyramid, all responsibilities are logically interlaced and the one that sits on the top of the pyramid feeds back into the economic and financial factors to contribute to the increase of the enterprise's profits. In other words, if society is satisfied with the philanthropy of the company, regardless of the exact activities and programmes that undergo, satisfaction will be transformed into support that in one way or another will have economic impact for the company.

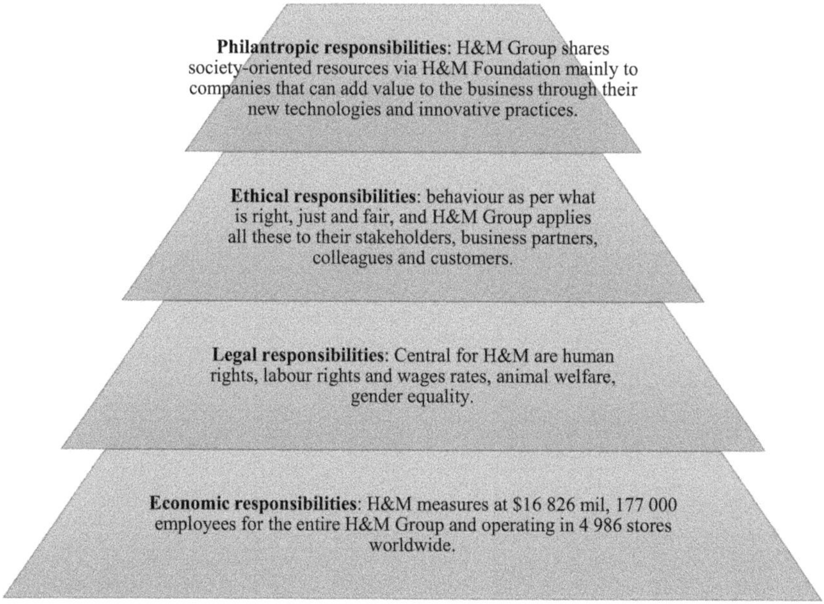

Philantropic responsibilities: H&M Group shares society-oriented resources via H&M Foundation mainly to companies that can add value to the business through their new technologies and innovative practices.

Ethical responsibilities: behaviour as per what is right, just and fair, and H&M Group applies all these to their stakeholders, business partners, colleagues and customers.

Legal responsibilities: Central for H&M are human rights, labour rights and wages rates, animal welfare, gender equality.

Economic responsibilities: H&M measures at $16 826 mil, 177 000 employees for the entire H&M Group and operating in 4 986 stores worldwide.

Figure 2. Carroll's pyramid model of Corporate Social Responsibility applied to H&M Group. Source: As per the researcher's collected data.

The impacts that H&M have along their value chain are very diverse due to the scale that the corporation operates in and are not only of economic importance. H&M alone scores more than 800 million customer transactions per year with products made in approximately 1670 factories located around the world. Therefore, the H&M Group differentiates seven areas of impact (see Table 3.), measuring it in percentage or narrative, depending on the data, assessment techniques and adopted national and global footprint methodologies (Ecofys, Water Footprint Network's methodology, etc.).

	Our influence	Climate impact	Water impact	Social impact
Design	High	0%	0%	Low
Raw materials	Medium	9%	87%	High
Fabric and yarn production	Medium	46%	6%	High
Product manufacturing	Medium	18%	1%	High
Transport	Medium	2%	0%	Low
Sales	High	0%	0%	High
Use	Low	21%	8%	Medium

Table 3. Impact areas of sustainability of H&M Group for 2017 and 2018. Source: H&M Website.

The organisation of the impacts clearly demonstrates *public responsibility* of H&M and their attempt to act in a circular way. Getting deeper into the essence of being publicly responsible though reveals the complexity of the task and the fact that a single company cannot change the whole industry on their own and perform all of its activities sustainably. Some changes require more than the company's will – legal changes worldwide are needed, the support and active involvement of national institutions, decision-makers, policy-makers, controlling agencies and the joint efforts of the entire industry. What H&M pledges to do is to accelerate these changes by looking for the achievement of shared responsibility and influencing the industry with their size and scale. It is not that the company transfers the responsibility elsewhere, but it intends to enhance the industry collaboration and secure systemic change across the whole fashion network. Furthermore, *legitimacy* is achieved by the continued commitment of H&M to the United Nations Global Impact and regular work with national governments and key stakeholders who would have the means to bring positive change by joint actions.

4.2 Current CSR practices and programmes

When reviewing the current CSR practices and programmes, it has become clear that *visibility and transparency* take huge part of H&M's CSR strategy. In the `XXI century the stakeholders and customers' expectations are centred around the requirement for companies to prove that they make sustainable choices as opposed to predominantly business and profit oriented decisions. For the corporations on the other hand, it is important to be open about the decisions they make and what necessitates those decisions, which can be viewed as controversial at times and get severely criticised. For example, this has been the case with the employee wages in supplier factories. Fast fashion producers, including big brands such as H&M, Zara, Nike, etc., are held accountable for maintaining non-ethical conduct regarding the wages of their workers in the supplier factories. Talking openly about the issue and trying to verbalise the context in which those companies operate in Asia and Latin America, the obstructions H&M and business partners face is already a way forward. Building trust, credibility and maintaining the dialogue with the respective decision-makers should be encountered as a considerable sustainable effort even if it is not exactly an immediate resolution of the existing problems in the fashion industry. The main challenge for corporations of the scale of H&M is the inability to maintain direct business relationship with suppliers of tier 2, 3 or beyond. Practically, this should be the case for small retailers too, but the pressure on them is far smaller and rarely held accountable at the same rate as fashion giants such as H&M and Zara. Illustratively, H&M would aspire to share information of the whole supply chain, starting from Garment production (Tier 1) and going through Fabric production

(Tier 2), Yarn spinning (Tier 3), Raw material sold at wholesale (Tier 4) to finish with Raw material sourcing (Tier 5).[62]

The study has found that two major customer-facing transparency programmes are going on at the moment, one being the H&M Conscious Exclusive Collection and the other one – the transparency business model of ARKET (one of the two latest brands belonging to the H&M Group). The H&M Conscious feature allows customers to find out the location where their clothes were made, the materials that were used and who was involved in making them. The functionality offered when visiting the ARKET website gives clients the opportunity to approach the issue in a different way. Instead of picking up a garment and learning about its origin, all ARKET products are searchable by the country of origin and material type. This way supplier information becomes customer-facing, easy to access and retrieve and with much more information on tier 1 suppliers available with only a few clicks. The entire process is sustainably oriented both ways – on one hand customers get in-depth look at the supplier and its production unit that has made the respective product, on the other hand, the supplier gets recognition for their joint work with H&M and considerable contribution to H&M's production.

The ability to gain benefits for the company understood as specificity can be exemplified with the H&M Foundation's Global Change Award, that has been going on annually since 2015. It is an initiative of H&M Group for newbies in innovation and technologies who would have the potential to accelerate H&M's attempts to become a fully circular fashion company and to lead the change for the entire industry to transform from linear to circular. Circular models function towards the concept of maximising resources and minimising waste and under the assumption that natural resources are running out. The winners of the Global

---

[62]H&M Group. Op. cit., 2017, p. 21.

Change Award receive financial support and exclusive access for an year to an innovation centre supported by the H&M Foundation, Accenture and KTH Royal Institute of Technology in Stockholm. As per the competition's rules, H&M Group does not take any equity or copyrights/intellectual property rights in the innovative ideas presented and competing in the event. For example, in 2017 the innovative projects that received funding had presented the following exclusive sustainable decisions:

- Grape Leather [Italy] – to use leftovers from the winemaking process to create leather that is completely of vegetal origin;
- Solar Textiles [US/Switzerland] – to harvest solar energy in order to produce fabrics for fashion products;
- Content Thread [US/UK] – to use a digital thread for sorting and recycling of clothing;
- Denim-dyed Denim [Australia] – dying new denim by using already used denim fabric;
- Manure Couture [the Netherlands] – to make cow manure-based fabric.

As visible from the selection of winners, the circular model is being applied holistically and into every stage of the H&M's value chain (Stage 1. Design; Stage 2. Material choice; Stage 3. Production processes; 4. Product use; 5. Product reuse and recycling) and it expands beyond the products and materials to include switching to renewable energy sources, cutting emissions and becoming a leader for positive transformation.

Responding to the global necessities requires the corporation to keep up to speed with all global events, trends and tendencies. The annual award is not the only initiative that proves H&M Group's *proactivity and ability to foresee social trends*. The initiative of H&M's brand Weekday in September 2017 (later repeated several times) to launch print projects that make connection to the most discussed and trendiest events in popular culture, politics and society demonstrated that H&M has taken sustainable position in relation with topics such as social media addiction, self-acceptance and image appreciation, women's rights, gender equality and mental health, that has come high on the agenda shortly beforehand.[63] The Cup Foundation activity is another example of sustainable behaviour that responds to the emerging dialogue around period and the need the stigma around it to end. The menstrual cups that were launched in Monki together with the brand Lunette showed H&M Group as proactive and philanthropic because part of the profits were directed towards supporting unprivileged girls in regions of the world where access to such toiletries and sanitary products is severely restricted with non-existing education on sexuality and reproduction.

H&M Group's policies that form its sustainable business strategy are organised on the basis of international equivalents and initiatives developed as part of International Labour Organisation Conventions and the United Nations Guiding Principles on Business and Human Rights. Several focus areas have been identified and the relevant standards applied to them to allow assessment:

- human rights throughout the value chain with applicable due diligence procedures in order to identify risks and adequately address before further deterioration;
- environment with assessments performed on a daily basis on water, chemicals, climate change, biodiversity and animal welfare;
- corruption;
- internal operations that put the code of ethics applicable to employees as priority complimented by global social policy, tax policy, etc.

---

[63]H&M Group. Op. cit., 2017, p. 77.

- business partners that are able to demonstrate sustainability as per the H&M Group official requirements;
- product and materials policies, where animal welfare chemical restrictions take priority over everything else in this area;

4.3 Empirical study of the existing CSR programmes in H&M

The empirical statistics section of the study is aimed to compliment the theoretical and critical analysis of the H&M's CSR and to test the study's hypothesis about the probability of existing positive dependence between the firm's CSR and customer behaviour, reflected in financial gains. To do so, the results of the conducted survey that has been tailored for the needs of the current research are compared to the data revealed by H&M Group in the beginning of 2019 in their latest sustainability report. The data extracted from the reports of H&M group is prepared on an annual basis (H&M Group's financial year that starts on 1 December and finishes on 30 November) in a transparent manner by addressing key impacts, regardless of their nature (including policies across the entire value chain and all brands with exception for franchise operations), scope (internal for H&M Group or external, including business partners and stakeholders) and characterisation (positive or negative). All the collected and published data by H&M Group on their CSR is reviewed by an internal for H&M Group controlling team of experts, applying a two-tier quality control principle.

Participants

In total 61 respondents answered to the invitation to get involved in the survey. 44 of them preferred to follow the link shared on two social media channels (Facebook and Workplace) and the rest responded by email. Figure 3. and Figure 4. present the participants' demographic profile, data for which has been derived from the first two questions of the survey: *'How old are you?'* and *'What is your gender?'*.

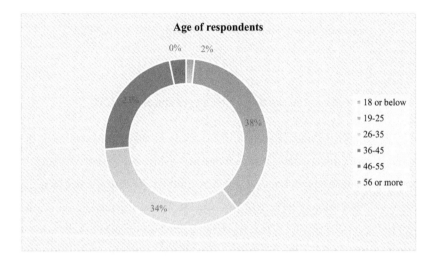

Figure 3. Age profile of the survey's respondents. Source: As per the researcher's collected data.

The participants aged between 19 and 35 years consist of 72% of the total people interviewed.

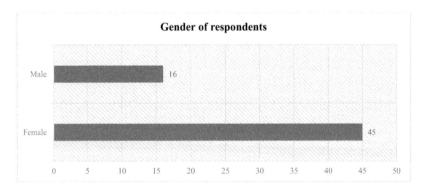

Figure 4. Gender profile of the survey's respondents. Source: As per the researcher's collected data.

Approximately 75% of the interviewees were female, which means that the findings and conclusions of this paper will be more relevant to women than men, if one would support the position that behaviour motivation with respect to CSR is triggered by gender.

The results of the demographic questions of the conducted survey would be comparable in the first place with the way H&M segments their customers. It needs to be clarified though that the segmentation is only applicable to the brand H&M and not to all brands included in H&M Group, because their target groups do not coincide. As it has been already explained, the survey is not nationality-oriented, which means segmentation by geographic areas would not be applicable on this occasion. Throughout the world H&M applies segmentation by class by offering apparel at low prices, therefore, targeting working lower middle class, including students.[64] Within the segment of lower middle class of working people, the branding of H&M is oriented mostly to women aging between 15 and 30 years (generation Y), who either still live at home, in student accommodation or in their first self-owned property. Generation Y characterises with ambitiousness, feminism and high buying drives and power, typically looking for affordable possibilities at more than one shopping outlet. Referring to the data in Figures 3. and 4., it is evident that the interviewed people match the targeted by H&M audience and their responses would have applicability and value for conducting the testing of the outlined hypothesis.

Although the survey does not provide more specific information than age and gender of the respondents, the description of the segmentation is enough to be deducted that it is most likely these young women to be subject to cultural, social and ethical influences shaping their lifestyle and personality. Supposedly, these customers are fashionable and treat the act of shopping as a type of outlet

---

[64]Delirium, Promille. Marketing Strategy H&M. Retrieved from
https://www.academia.edu/12881172/Marketing_Strategy_H_and_M

that allows them to relax and have enjoyable experiences in their daily lives, often shared with peers and family. The main issue with the target groups applied to the essence of the study is around the decision-making process that they are likely to follow, considering that it is most probable that the H&M's typical customer follows routine response behaviour expressed in frequently buying products and services at low cost with little previous research done and limited decision time, almost impulsively and often triggered by information on ongoing sales and exceptionally low prices as compared to the direct competitors. This means that it is unlikely that customers would have considered the aspect of social responsibility when making the purchase.

Procedures and measures

The survey was distributed online through Facebook, using the Google Forms platform. Participants were invited to share their perception and opinion regarding CSR as a whole and in relevance to H&M. Questions 3 to 6 (see Figure 5., Figure 6., Figure 7. and Figure 8.) of the questionnaire aim to clarify the level of knowledge and importance of CSR as a whole, without specifying on an enterprise.

The responses to the first question of the CSR general knowledge sequence are important as they are being used to build the foundation for interpreting the level of CSR importance to the customer and the generalisation of the answers received links with the previously outlined deduction that H&M customers are unlikely to be particularly interested in the company's social responsibility when making the purchase. Only 20% of the respondents do not have any knowledge about the sustainability policy included in the retail industry and another 23% have shared to have limited knowledge about it (see Figure 5.). Conservatively approached, that leaves the company with only 57% of customers to attract and retain on the basis of their social and environmental responsibility programmes.

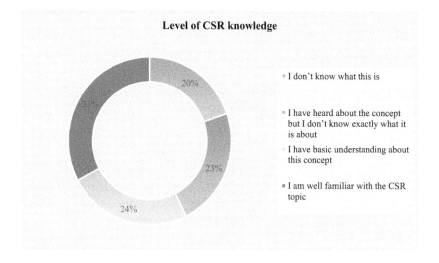

Level of CSR knowledge

- I don't know what this is
- I have heard about the concept but I don't know exactly what it is about
- I have basic understanding about this concept
- I am well familiar with the CSR topic

20%
23%
24%

Figure 5. Level of knowledge regarding CSR. Source: As per the researcher's collected data.

The results of the next question about what makes a company responsible have not distinguished any of the proposed answers as leading (see Figure 6.).

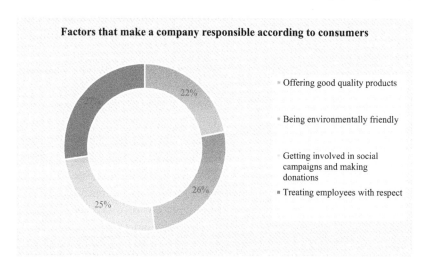

Factors that make a company responsible according to consumers

- Offering good quality products
- Being environmentally friendly
- Getting involved in social campaigns and making donations
- Treating employees with respect

22%
26%
25%

By checking the key CSR achievements of H&M Group for 2018, one can see that all of the key and commonly shared factors for a company to qualify as sustainable indeed appear in relation to the H&M Group (see Table 4.).

Key factors	Sustainability key achievements 2018
Offering good quality products	57% of all materials (95% of cotton) used to make garments are recycled or sustainably sourced; Customers are being offered guidance in some of the markets in how to take care of their clothing and therefore extend their life; Investing in innovative companies such as Moral Fiber and Colorifix
Being environmentally friendly	Development and getting approval of the 2030 GHG emissions reduction goals; Introducing a new circular packaging strategy for the entire value chain; Scored 16% increase in the amount of collected textiles for recycling and reuse; Developed a new Water Roadmap initiative
Getting involved in social campaigns and making donations	H&M introduced a tool that offer customers the opportunity to trace most of the products to the factory they have been produced to enable them to make a conscious and well-informed decisions; H&M Group is within Top 5 for corporations in fashion driving revolutionary practices;

	Reached the highest possible score in the category for Social Reporting of the Dow Jones Sustainability Index
Treating employees with respect	655 factories and 930,000 workers are included in programmes for workplace dialogue and Wage Management Systems

Table 4.Factors that have shaped the social responsibility of H&M Group in 2018. Source: H&M Sustainability Report 2018.

Cross-referencing with the H&M Group's Sustainability Report for 2018 indicated that making donations in the traditional meaning of the activity does not actually happen and it is balanced out by involvement of social campaigns that are somehow connected to fashion, but never outside of it. However, scoring high as per the Dow Jones Sustainability Index could be taken into consideration for providing credibility that the corporation gets involved in social campaigns and that satisfies the customers and the company's stakeholders and partners. 'Treating employees with respect' is not as strongly presented in the section of the key achievements for the year, but that is not indicative enough to be assumed that the company does not do enough in this area.

The next question in the survey that looks at the attention paid to a company's CSR policy when making a purchase can easily be the most important for the entire research since proving of the hypothesis is dependent on it. The responses to the question in Figure 7. are consequential of those of the query in Figure 5. where respondents categorised their knowledge of CSR. The people who said that CSR is not important to them when making a purchase are likely to have responded in the way they did because they do not recognise the meaning of the policy and what it entails and not because they do not necessarily care for the values and the sustainability mission adopted by the company.

It should not be excluded that the assumption that the majority of respondents who think that CSR is not crucial, but desirable for a company may not fully understand how that CSR policy or concrete actions affect them. Reading through the sustainability report, it requires previous knowledge and in-depth research to appreciate the efforts H&M Group is making with regard to environmentally responsible behaviour. For example, by saying that H&M Group developed "a new roadmap for our supply chain which contains our key goals and actions up until 2022.", it is way too vague for even the most committed customers to make sense how this would affect them. At times, the language around the CSR strategy has not been elaborated and that may discourage the customer to prefer H&M to other brands only because of their sustainability measures.

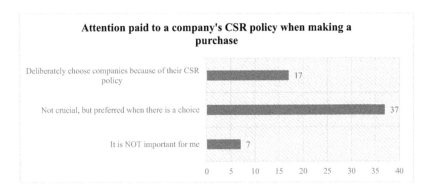

Figure 7. Attention paid to a company's CSR and the importance of its policy when a consumer is making a purchase. Source: As per the researcher's collected data.

Reviewing the H&M's Sustainability Report for 2017 in the interview with the company's Head of Sustainability, it becomes clear that the CSR strategy of H&M was not sporadically created, but very carefully crafted with the support of leading experts in the field with great knowledge of the challenges faced by the fashion industry. In the interview with Nanna Andersen, Head of H&M CO:LAB, published in the same sustainability report, it is explicitly said that some of the

CSR investments the corporation does are loaded with the expectation for financial return and development of the "business in a positive way."[65]Therefore, it does not come as a surprise that 10% of the respondents consider the income increase factor to be the leading one for companies to get involved in CSR activities (see Figure 8.).

The analysis of the sustainability information that H&M Group makes available to the general public has showed that financial data linking the CSR activities with the corporation's income almost lacks and there are barely any economic pointers to the profitability and the production of the firm that have come as a result of the implemented sustainability strategy. Indirectly related numbers to CSR that are however included in the annual report present the figure of net sales (incl. VAT), that has changed from 232 billion Swedish kronor in 2017 to 210 billion Swedish kronor and the figure for H&M alone customer transactions per year – 800 million in 2017 and the same in 2018.

---

[65]H&M Group. Op. cit., 2017, p. 19.

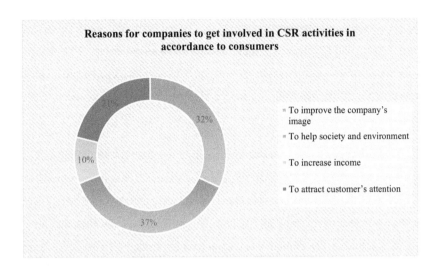

Reasons for companies to get involved in CSR activities in accordance to consumers

- To improve the company's image
- To help society and environment
- To increase income
- To attract customer's attention

32%
10%
37%

Figure 8. Reasons for companies to get involved in CSR activities in accordance to consumers. Source: As per the researcher's collected data.

The opinion of respondents that companies choose to adopt CSR policies into their strategies in order to improve their image has been widely discussed for a while by business experts and customer satisfaction analysts due to the complexity of branding in the 21st century. Giants in fashion industry such as H&M are constantly subject to critics because of their fast fashion methods and the negative consequences that are brought to society, mainly the harmful impact to the environment. But even when elaborate CSR programmes are put in place, they get scrutinised all the time for inadequacies and that is mainly because of the popularity of the brand and the naturally attracted interest onto its functioning. So it is questionable if a CSR can effectively contribute to the brand's image and if yes, for how long the positive impact will last to really have an effect on customer behaviour towards the brand. For example, in 2018 H&M Group reported that 20 649 tonnes of textiles were collected to be reused or recycled. When the information was presented to customers, undoubtedly the image of the brand has improved to be seen as a pro-active and sustainable fashion influencer.

However, a documentary shared in media in 2017 has impacted negatively H&M's image when it showed that nearly 12 tonnes of the collected and unsold by H&M clothing were burnt.[66] It remains speculative how much a CSR can improve a company's image and whether this could be the approach for a firm whose image has been suffering with bad reputation, but whichever of the two it is, there is no doubt that customer's attention is attracted only by the mentioning of Corporate Social Responsibility.

The last two questions in the survey are H&M specific – '*Do you recognise H&M as a responsible company?*' and '*Have you ever heard of any of the following activities that H&M undertake to be socially and environmentally responsible?.*' Figure 9. visualises the proportion of respondents who recognise H&M as being responsible to those who would not associate the brand with responsible practices. Although the Ethisphere Institute has named H&M as one of the companies with the strongest ethical responsibilities globally, only half of the interviewed people would agree with the institute's statement.[67]

Recognition of H&M as a responsible company

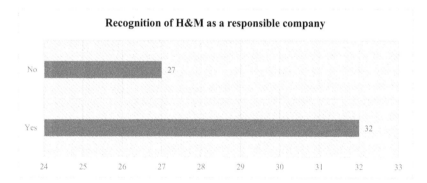

[66]Farmbrough, Heather. H&M Is Pushing Sustainability Hard, But Not Everyone is Convinced. Forbes Website, 2018. Retrieved from https://www.forbes.com/sites/heatherfarmbrough/2018/04/14/hm-is-pushing-sustainability-hard-but-not-everyone-is-convinced/#65cf139e7ebd
[67]Ethisphere Institute. The 2019 World's Most Ethical Companies: Honoree List, 2019. Retrieved from http://www.worldsmostethicalcompanies.com/honorees/

Figure 9. Recognition of H&M as a responsible company. Source: As per the researcher's collected data.

The last question in the survey seeks to find out which of the CSR campaigns are getting recognition among customers and potentially benefit H&M in achieving their financial, strategic and sustainability KPIs. As suggested in the very beginning of the research, the initiative that is the most popular one among all SCR activities is the recycling programme of the H&M Group, which consists in collecting used garments and forwarding them to be reused or recycled (see Figure 10.). For every bag of donated garments for recycling, customers get a voucher for discount to use next time when they make a purchase from the brand. The goal the H&M Group has set up is by 2020 to have 25 000 tonnes of garments collected through their initiatives – for reference in 2018 they collected nearly 21 000 tonnes and the programme is currently running in 63% of their stores worldwide.[68]

---

[68]H&M Group. Op. cit., 2018, p. 32.

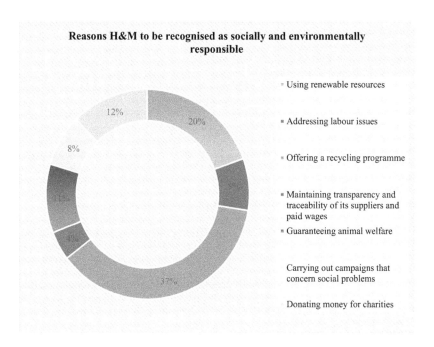

Reasons H&M to be recognised as socially and environmentally responsible

- Using renewable resources
- Addressing labour issues
- Offering a recycling programme
- Maintaining transparency and traceability of its suppliers and paid wages
- Guaranteeing animal welfare

Carrying out campaigns that concern social problems

Donating money for charities

Figure 10. Reasons H&M to be recognised as socially and environmentally responsible according to the respondents. Source: As per the researcher's collected data.

Using renewable resources comes second as per the respondents' answers and this result feeds into the H&M Group's objective to become a circular and renewable corporation by 2030 at the latest with 100% of recycled or other sustainably sourced materials of total material use for commercial goals. In 2015 H&M Group measured at 20% to achieve the set goal, increased it to 26% in 2016, 35% in 2017 and up to 57% in 2018.[69] The data shows that H&M Group performed extremely well and has the potential to influence the sector towards social and environmental changes in areas such as becoming climate positive by creating energy-efficient garments made of sustainable material and improving

[69]Ibid.

supply chains with the increasing use of renewable and sustainable energy, decreasing emissions and reduced energy needs as a whole.

Next among the reasons H&M to be recognised as socially and environmentally responsible is donating money to charities, followed by guaranteeing animal welfare, addressing labour issues and carrying out campaigns that concern social problems. The reason that is the least recognised in relation to H&M's CSR strategy is being transparent and traceable in its relationships with suppliers and the wages paid to employees.

These results project H&M in a slightly different light compared to the image the company aims to create among its target audiences. H&M sources its virgin wool only from Responsible Wool Standard certified farms and by 2020 mohair will be phased out completely from the company's products, however, those fabrics represent a small share of the total material use at H&M. In other words, the animal welfare approach exists, but its small fraction of the overall produce of H&M makes it an insignificant initiative. The same is applicable to the reasoning that H&M is responsible because it donates money to charities, when the company rarely makes direct donations and in most cases they come as a consequence of customer behaviour, donating money on their behalf after having purchased a specific product. The opposite is the situation with the understanding of customers about H&M's efforts to maintain transparent and traceable responsibilities to employees, especially with regard to their wages. Customers feel that this is almost a weakness of H&M and does not create positive association when considering the brand's CSR, while the corporation has been putting considerable efforts to lead the change in thefashion industry by signing partnership agreements with ILO and covering 655 of the tier 1 and tier 2 factories by the key programmes for workplace dialogues and Wage

Management Systems.[70] Furthermore, in 2018 the H&M Group hosted an event in Phnom Penh to share impact, findings and learnings from its work with experts, trade unions, suppliers and NGOs on the Fair Living Wage Strategy. The 2018 Ethical Fashion Report also praised H&M for their commendable improvements on labour policies in past years and assessed the company with the top score of "A+" for its Supplier Code of Conduct (that is only applicable to part of the value chain).[71] At the same time, the name of the company appeared in the 2018 report of Global Labour Justice with reference to abuse of female garment employees, which shadowed the definite progress of H&M since 2013 when the firm had made its commitment to address labour issues in the entire production chain.[72]

---

[70] H&M Group. Op. cit., 2018, p. 61.
[71] Baptist World Aid Australia. 2018 Ethical Fashion Report, 2018. Retrieved from
https://baptistworldaid.org.au/resources/2019-ethical-fashion-report/
[72] Robertson, Lara. How Ethical Is H&M? Good on You Website, 2019. Retrieved from
https://goodonyou.eco/how-ethical-is-hm/

V. CONCLUSION

Reviewing the Corporate Social Responsibility of the world's second largest fashion producer, the research concludes that despite the prominent sustainability targets and ongoing positive practices across the board, with the ultimate goal to minimise any harm on society and instead, enlarge the beneficial impact to involve a wider circle of audiences, H&M's CSR remains considerably controversial and not acknowledged by likely half of its customers. Partially, the reasoning behind this is the fact that H&M remains a brand that designs garments with short lifespan and with its business goals, it contributes to the unsustainable fast fashion industry.

The analysis of the company's situation of its efforts to manage CSR in the highly-competitive, global environment, in which the retailer exists contributed to formulating the following findings:

- H&M has a wide range of social responsibility practices to qualify as sustainable in all four factors that it has been tested against - offering good quality products, being environmentally friendly, getting involved in social campaigns and making donations and treating employees with respect. However, the research has not found any proof of H&M to have made donations in the traditional meaning of the activity.
- The probability respondents to not fully understand the CSR efforts made by H&M through their production work is assessed to be medium to high, especially considering that more than 50% of the respondents have stated that they do not find it crucial when making their decision. Furthermore, the study has found that the language used to describe CSR activities

requires previous knowledge on the subject and often it is not transcribed into language accessible to general public.

- Despite being widely recognised by researchers and experts in the field for its CSR oriented efforts, H&M is recognised by customers as socially and environmentally responsible only by half of its customers.

- The recycling programme of H&M is the most recognised sustainable action of the retailer by its customers, while the results with reference to its other activities remain ambiguous.

- Even if 20% of the respondents stated that they do not have any prior knowledge of what CSR is, approximately only 10% of them admitted that CSR does not hold any importance to them when they are shopping. Due to the fixed response questions, certain discrepancies of data have been generated, which impacts the credibility of the survey results and poses limitations to the outlined findings, decreasing their probability and requiring further research.

The paper's findings by all means do not present fully conclusive information and are subject to certain limitations, but still provide checkable and reliably derived data that CSR policies do not fully define the behaviour of H&M's customers and it is one of the low to medium key factors that motivate them when making a purchase. The assumption that the most popular sustainability initiative of the brand would be one that generates direct value to its customers gets proved – that is, the recycling initiative of H&M which offers a voucher of 15% off of their next H&M purchase for every bag of unwanted garments and textiles the customer brings in-store for recycling, re-wear and reuse.

In order for the findings and conclusions of the current research to be put into perspective, further study of the fast fashion industry needs to be carried out to compare how the other corporations of the scale of H&M perform to meet the

CSR expectations of customers, stakeholders and business partners. In-depth analysis of the joint initiatives the retail industry undertakes would give a clearer picture of the challenges the fashion retailers face and how successful each enterprise is in managing them, respectively how that is appreciated by customers and if it has a positive effect on their customer satisfaction and loyalty. All these aspects make CSR highly applicable in all forms of business development and most importantly crucial for increasing the responsible and sustainable behaviour in such a resource-intensive industry like the clothing and textile production.

VI. LIST OF REFERENCES

Agudelo, Mauricio Andrés Latapí, Jóhannsdóttir, Lára and Davídsdóttir, Brynhildur. A literature review of the history and evolution of corporate social responsibility. // International Journal of Corporate Social Responsibility, 2019, 4:1, pp. 1-23.

Anderson, Eugene W. and Mittal, Vikas. Strengthening the satisfaction-profit chain. // Journal of Service Research, 2000, 3 (2), pp. 107–120.

Baptist World Aid Australia. 2018 Ethical Fashion Report, 2018. Retrieved from https://baptistworldaid.org.au/resources/2019-ethical-fashion-report/

Bhattacharya, C. B., and Sen, Sankar. Consumer-company identification: A framework for understanding consumers' relationships with companies. // Journal of Marketing, 2003, 67 (2), pp. 76–88.

Bowen, Howard R. Social responsibilities of the businessman. University of Iowa Press, 1953.

Brown, Tom J. and Dacin, Peter A. The Company and the Product: Corporate Associations and Consumer Product Responses. // Journal of Marketing, 1997, Vol. 61, No. 1, pp. 68-84.

Burke, Lee, and Logsdon, Jeanne M. How corporate social responsibility pays off. // Long Range Planning, 1996, 29 (4), pp. 495–502.

Carroll, Archie B. A three-dimensional conceptual model of corporate performance. // Academy of management review, 1979, 4 (4), pp. 497–505.

Carroll, Archie B. A history of corporate social responsibility: concepts and practices. In A. M. Andrew Crane, D. Matten, J. Moon and D. Siegel

(Eds.), The Oxford handbook of corporate social responsibility (pp. 19–46). New York, Oxford University Press, 2008.

Carroll, Archie B. Corporate social responsibility: The centerpiece of competing and complementary frameworks. // Organizational Dynamics, 2015, 44 (2), pp. 87–96.

Chaffee, Eric C. The Origins of Corporate Social Responsibility. // University of Cincinnati Law Review, 2017, Vol. 85. Retrieved from SSRN: https://ssrn.com/abstract=2957820

CSR Europe. CSR Europe - 20 years of business-policy interaction driving the CSR movement. CSR Europe Website, 2016. Retrieved from https://www.csreurope.org/history

Delirium, Promille. Marketing Strategy H&M. Retrieved from https://www.academia.edu/12881172/Marketing_Strategy_H_and_M

Du Pisani, Jacobus A. Sustainable development – historical roots of the concept. // Environmental Sciences, 2006, 3 (2), pp. 83-96.

Ethisphere Institute. The 2019 World's Most Ethical Companies: Honoree List, 2019. Retrieved from http://www.worldsmostethicalcompanies.com/honorees/

European Commission. Communication from the Commission to the European Parliament, the Council, the European Economic and Social Committee and the Committee of the Regions: A renewed EU strategy 2011-14 for Corporate Social Responsibility. Brussels, COM 2011, 681 final. Retrieved fromhttps://www.employment.gov.sk/files/slovensky/ministerstvo/spoloc enska-zodpovednost/new-communication-on-csr-2011-2014.pdf

European Commission. Corporate social responsibility: a new definition, a new agenda for action. (MEMO/11/732, MEMO/11/734 and MEMO/11/735). European Commission Website, 2011. Retrieved from http://europa.eu/rapid/press-release_MEMO-11-730_en.htm

European Commission. Industry: Corporate Social Responsibility & Responsible Business Conduct. European Commission Website, 2011. Retrieved fromhttps://ec.europa.eu/growth/industry/corporate-social-responsibility_en

Farmbrough, Heather. H&M Is Pushing Sustainability Hard, But Not Everyone is Convinced. Forbes Website, 2018. Retrieved from https://www.forbes.com/sites/heatherfarmbrough/2018/04/14/hm-is-pushing-sustainability-hard-but-not-everyone-is-convinced/#65cf139e7ebd

Ferreira, Aristides I. and Ribeiro, Inês. Are you willing to pay the price? The impact of corporate social (ir)responsibility on consumer behaviour towards national and foreign brands. //Journal of Consumer Behaviour, 2017, 16, pp. 63 – 71.

Frederick, William. The growing concern over business responsibility. // California Management Review, 1960, 2 (4), pp. 54–61.

Friedman, Milton. Capitalism and freedom. United States of America, University of Chicago Press, 1962.

Jakštienė,Sandra, Susnienė. Daliaand Narbutas, Valdas. The Psychological Impact of Advertising on the Consumer Behaviour. // Communications of the IBIMA, 2008,No. 3, pp. 50-55. Retrieved from https://ibimapublishing.com/articles/CIBIMA/2008/521523/521523.pdf

Jones, Thomas. Corporate social responsibility revisited, redefined. // California Management Review, 1980, 22 (3), pp. 59–67.

Harrison, Brian. Philanthropy and the Victorians. // Victorian Studies, 1966, 9(4), pp. 353–374.

H&M. Our History: The H&M group – the first 70 years. H&M Website, 2017. Retrieved from https://about.hm.com/content/dam/hmgroup/groupsite/documents/en/Digital%20Annual%20Report/2017/Annual%20Report%202017%20Our%20history.pdf

H&M Group. Sustainability Report 2017, 2017. Retrieved from https://about.hm.com/content/dam/hmgroup/groupsite/documents/masterlanguage/CSR/reports/2017%20Sustainability%20report/HM_group_SustainabilityReport_2017_FullReport.pdf

H&M Group. Sustainability Report 2018, 2018. Retrieved from https://about.hm.com/content/dam/hmgroup/groupsite/documents/masterlanguage/CSR/reports/2018_Sustainability_report/HM_Group_SustainabilityReport_2018_%20FullReport.pdf

Interbrand. Best Global Brands 2018 Ranking: H&M, 2019. Retrieved from https://www.interbrand.com/best-brands/best-global-brands/2018/ranking/hm/

Lantos, Geoffrey P. The boundaries of strategic corporate social responsibility. // Journal of Consumer Marketing, 2001, 18(7), pp. 595–632.

Levine, David M., Berenson, Mark L. and Stephan, David. Statistics for managers using Microsoft Excel (Vol. 660). Upper Saddle River, New Jersey, Prentice Hall, 2008.

Lindgreen, A., Xu, Y., Maon, F., and Wilcock, J. Corporate social responsibility brand leadership: A multiple case study. // European Journal of Marketing, 2012, 46 (7/8), pp. 965–993.

Maignan, Isabelle. Consumers' perceptions of corporate social responsibilities: a cross-cultural comparison. // Journal of Business Ethics, 2001, 30 (1), pp. 57-72.

Maignan, Isabelle and Ferrell, O. C. Measuring Corporate Citizenship in Two Countries: The Case of the United States and France. // Journal of Business Ethics 2000, 23, pp. 283-297.

Mälstad, Sofie and Byström, Carin. Consumers' Perception of CSR within the Fashion Industry. Luleå University of Technology, 2013.

Oliver, Richard L. Satisfaction: A behavioral perspective on the consumer (2nd Ed.). New York, M.E. Sharpe, 2010.

Öberseder, Magdalena, Schlegelmilch, Bobo B. and Gruber, Verena. "Why Don't Consumers Care About CSR?": A Qualitative Study Exploring the Role of CSR in Consumption Decisions. // Journal of Business Ethics, 2011, 104, pp. 449-460.

Pomering, Alan and Dolnicar, Sara. Assessing the prerequisite of successful csr implementation: Are consumers aware of CSR initiatives? // Journal of Business Ethics, 2009, 85 (Suppl. 2), pp. 285–301.

Porter, Michael and Kramer, Mark. Creating shared value. // Harvard Business Review 2011, (January-February).

Rawwas, Mohommed Y. A. Culture, personality and morality: A typology of international consumers' ethical beliefs. // International Marketing Review, , 2001, 18 (2), pp. 188- 211.

Robertson, Lara. How Ethical Is H&M? Good on You Website, 2019. Retrieved from https://goodonyou.eco/how-ethical-is-hm/

Sen, Sankar and Bhattacharya, C. B. Does Doing Good Always Lead to Doing Better? Consumer Reactions to Corporate Social Responsibility. // Journal of Marketing Research, 2001, 38, pp. 225-243.

Smith, Craig. Changes in corporate practices in response to public interest advocacy and actions. In P. N. B. a. G. T. Gundlach (Ed.), Handbook of Marketing and Society. Thousand Oaks, 2001.

Socially Responsible Causes Ben & Jerry's Has Advocated for. Ben & Jerry's Website, 2014. Retrieved fromhttps://www.benjerry.com/whats-new/2014/corporate-social-responsibility-history

Sprinkle, Geoffrey B., and Maines, Laureen A. The benefits and costs of corporate social responsibility. // Business Horizons, 2010, 53 (5), pp. 445–453.

Trapp, N. Leila Corporation as climate ambassador: Transcending business sector boundaries in a Swedish CSR campaign. // Public Relations Review, 2012, 38 (3), pp. 458–465.

Tsarenko, Yelena and Tojib, Dewi. Consumers' forgiveness after brand transgression: the effect of the firm's corporate social responsibility and response. // Journal of Marketing Management, 2015, Vol. 31, Nos. 17-18, pp. 1851-1877.

Tuzzolino, F. and Armandi, B. R. A need-hierarchy framework for assessing corporate social responsibility. The Academy of Management Review, 1981, 6 (1), pp. 21–28.

Unruh, Gregory. No, Consumers Will Not Pay More for Green. The CSR Blog Contributor Group, Forbes Website, 2011. Retrieved fromhttps://www.forbes.com/sites/csr/2011/07/28/no-consumers-will-not-pay-more-for-green/#6c71a1703b28

Walton, Clarence. Corporate Social responsibilities. United States of America, Wadsworth Publishing Company, 1967.

Wood, Donna J. Corporate social performance revisited. // The Academy of Management Review, 1991, 16 (4), pp. 691–718.

Yuen, Kum Fai, Thai, Vinh V. and Wong, Yiik Diew.Are customers willing to pay for corporate social responsibility? A study of individual-specific mediators. // Total Quality Management, 2016, Vol. 27, No. 8, pp. 912-926.

VII. ANNEX I. CSR H&M Survey (English version)

1. How old are you?

- 18 or below
- 19-25
- 26-35
- 36-45
- 45-55
- 56 or more

2. What is your gender?

- Female
- Male

3. What is the level of your knowledge regarding Corporate Social Responsibility (CSR)?

- I don't know what this is
- I have heard about the concept but I don't know exactly what it is about
- I have basic understanding about this concept
- I am well familiar with the CSR topic

4. What makes a company responsible in your opinion?

- Offering good quality products
- Being environmentally friendly
- Getting involved in social campaigns and making donations
- Treating employees with respect

5. How much attention do you pay to the CSR policy of a company as a customer?

- It is NOT important for me
- It is not crucial for me, but when I have a choice, I prefer companies that are responsible
- I deliberately choose companies which I recognize as being responsible

6. What are the most important reasons for companies to get involved in CSR activities in your opinion?

- To improve the company's image
- To help society and the environment
- To increase income

- To attract customer's attention

7. Do you recognise H&M as a responsible company?

- Yes
- No

8. Have you ever heard of any of the following activities that H&M undertakes to be socially and environmentally responsible?

- Using renewable resources
- Addressing labour issues
- Offering a recycling programme
- Maintaining transparency and traceability of its suppliers and paid wages
- Guaranteeing animal welfare
- Carrying out campaigns that concern social problems
- Donating money for charities

Milton Keynes UK
Ingram Content Group UK Ltd.
UKHW040756020224
437154UK00004B/234